IMAGES
of America

HISTORIC HOTELS
AND MOTELS
OF THE OUTER BANKS

ON THE COVER: The Cavalier Motor Court was the first Outer Banks motel built in the motor court style, in which vehicles entered on one side of the property and exited on the other. Construction on the 19-unit motel began in 1949, and owner Roy Wescott Sr. opened it on Memorial Day weekend 1950. Now known as The Cavalier By The Sea, the motel has 54 units and continues to welcome new and repeat guests, some of whom have been returning each year for more than half a century. (Courtesy of Dale Wescott.)

IMAGES of America
HISTORIC HOTELS AND MOTELS OF THE OUTER BANKS

Elizabeth Ownley Cooper

ARCADIA
PUBLISHING

Copyright © 2020 by Elizabeth Ownley Cooper
ISBN 978-1-4671-0487-6

Published by Arcadia Publishing
Charleston, South Carolina

Library of Congress Control Number: 2019954253

For all general information, please contact Arcadia Publishing:
Telephone 843-853-2070
Fax 843-853-0044
E-mail sales@arcadiapublishing.com
For customer service and orders:
Toll-Free 1-888-313-2665

Visit us on the Internet at www.arcadiapublishing.com

DEDICATION. This book is dedicated to my parents, Bob and Ann Ownley, who began their marriage by opening The Vacationer Motel and who instilled in me the values of faith, hard work, integrity, and perseverance. Pictured above are Bob, Ann, and Beth Ownley on the grounds of The Vacationer Motel in the summer of 1966. (Author's collection.)

Contents

Acknowledgments		6
Introduction		7
1.	The Grand Dames	9
2.	Nags Head	27
3.	Kill Devil Hills	67
4.	Kitty Hawk	89
5.	Roanoke Island	95
6.	Hatteras Island	105
7.	Ocracoke Island	117

Acknowledgments

Many thanks go to everyone who contributed to this book. I appreciate the time each of you took to share photographs and stories of your family businesses with me. Thank you for helping to preserve a vital piece of Outer Banks history.

Special thanks to Melodye Cannady, Lara Carter, Trudy Clark, Wanda Daniels, Dave Dawson, Carol Dillon, Bill and Cari Foreman, Wayne Garrish, Pam Gladden, Elizabeth Granitzki, Jill Gunter, Margaret Harvey, Cyndy Mann Holda, Annette Rogers Jackson, David and Maryann Maryott, Rodney Minton, Tomek Pakula, Bill Rapant, April Ross, Alexandra Miller Saunders, Susan Sawin, Elizabeth Thompson Seawell, Dale Wescott, and Bebe Woody, who pulled together information and photographs about their family hotels and motels to share with me. Also, Angie Brady-Daniels and Nancy Gray offered advice and insight as I tackled this project, and Sydney Nolan shared her editing expertise in reviewing the copy.

This book could not have been completed without the assistance of Tama Creef and Stuart Parks, archivists at the Outer Banks History Center, who gave me access to the center's large collection of historic photographs and other materials and patiently answered my questions.

Thank you also to the staff at the Ocracoke Preservation Society for helping me uncover historic photographs and information about Ocracoke's historic lodging establishments.

Members of the Outer Banks Vintage Scrapbook page on Facebook contributed information about many long-gone hotels and motels that helped shape the region and remain firmly rooted in our memories.

My husband, Michael Cooper, encouraged me to take on this project and provided invaluable technical assistance. I could not have done this without his support.

My children, Bobby, Jeffrey, and Juliana Cooper, also encouraged me as I worked on this book. I appreciate their interest and questions and hope they will cherish the book as part of their family legacy.

Unless otherwise noted, all images are courtesy of the Outer Banks History Center.

Introduction

Salt air, sand, and sea, not to mention vanished settlers, the first man-powered airplane, lighthouses, and a pirate known for his bushy black beard, have long drawn visitors to North Carolina's Outer Banks. To accommodate them, entrepreneurs over the years opened a variety of lodging establishments on this strip of barrier islands. From mom-and-pop motels to full-service hotels, as well as cottage courts and tourist homes, these facilities added to the area's colorful history.

The Outer Banks first became a tourist destination in the 1830s, when wealthy farmers and businessmen from Pasquotank, Perquimans, Chowan, Bertie, and Washington Counties, as well as southeastern Virginia, brought their families to Nags Head via boat to escape the summer heat. The first hotel, known as the Ocean Retreat, opened on the sound side near Jockey's Ridge in June 1841 and soon became the center of the fledgling resort's social life. By 1851, the hotel had expanded to more than 200 guest rooms, several cottages, a dining room, a ballroom, a general store, a steamer wharf, a boardwalk, and a horse-drawn railroad that transported guests to the beach.

That carefree summer existence ended when the Civil War encroached upon the Outer Banks. In 1862, Confederate general Henry A. Wise used the hotel as his headquarters, but after Union general Ambrose Burnside led his troops to victory in the Battle of Roanoke Island, Wise and his men hastily retreated, setting fire to the hotel to keep it from falling into enemy hands.

In 1866, A.E. Jacobs, one of the investors in the Ocean Retreat, rebuilt the hotel, naming it the Alexina House. The 200-foot-long, two-story hotel featured a piazza that wound around the entire building. A horse-drawn railroad transported guests from the Alexina's pier to Ocean Beach, a pavilion on the "Sea Beach," and three restaurants on Roanoke Sound. An 1886 newspaper ad promoted an abundance of cistern water for drinking.

Another soundside lodging establishment, the Nag's Head Hotel, opened in July 1873. The three-story, 100-room hotel featured a 10-pin bowling alley and nightly square dancing in the dining room. Passengers disembarked from steamers onto a wharf and traveled to the oceanfront aboard the Nags Head Railway, a horse and wagon run over wooden tracks on the sand.

After the Alexina was abandoned due to encroaching sand, Jacobs took over the Nag's Head Hotel in 1884 and sold it at a public auction in 1889. John Z. Lowe of Norfolk, Virginia, owned and operated the hotel until it was destroyed by fire in July 1903. The tragedy was compounded by the death of Lowe's wife, Quill Ella Jenkins Lowe, who suffered a heart attack during the blaze.

Although the hotel-chartered steamer stopped running after the fire, other steamers ferried visitors to the sand-swept shores, along with the sailboat *Hattie Creef*, which transported Wilbur and Orville Wright to the Outer Banks to test their flying machine. Traveling by steamboat from Elizabeth City to Nags Head in the early 1900s typically took more than four hours.

Upon arriving at Nags Head, visitors either stayed in cottages along the sound or in hotels, including Graham Hollowell's namesake hotel (later known as the Pleasant View Hotel), which he opened in 1910, and the 24-room Albemarle Cottage, which opened in 1912 at approximately the same spot where the Nag's Head Hotel had stood. The Albemarle Cottage was destroyed during a March 1933 storm.

In the early 1920s, the North Carolina General Assembly allocated $50 million for highway construction across the state. By 1932, North Carolina Highway 12 was completed. The 18-mile road ran from the Roanoke Sound Bridge in Nags Head to the Wright Memorial Bridge, which had opened in September 1930. Improved access to the area led to a steady influx of visitors, and tourism grew throughout the decade, with 1939 being the largest season in the Outer Banks' history. Hotels of this era were simple wooden structures. Most were built on pilings and featured wide porches where guests enjoyed cooling ocean breezes.

More lodging establishments sprang up in the post–World War II building boom. By 1950, there were 10 hotels able to accommodate more than 1,000 guests and 14 motor courts with rooms for 930 visitors dotting the Outer Banks coastline. To help visitors find their way, the Beaches Chamber of Commerce spent $176 in 1950 to erect mile markers along Virginia Dare Trail between the Wright Memorial Bridge and the Roanoke Sound Bridge.

By the late 1960s, more than 150 hotels, motels, motor courts, guesthouses, and cottage courts provided accommodations for visitors traveling to the Outer Banks. Most were independent and locally owned, hosting travelers from all 50 states and around the world. Many visitors returned at the same time each year, forming friendships with their fellow guests and with the motel proprietors.

Although these family-run businesses were instrumental in the Outer Banks' evolution as one of the world's most popular vacation destinations, their number has dwindled significantly over the past several decades. Since the mid-1990s, numerous old-school motels have become victims of the wrecking ball, often replaced by grand beach cottages able to house groups of 20 or more people. Others continue to hang on, even enjoying a rebirth of sorts as more visitors desire to return to a simpler era when a luxurious vacation involved staying in a motel with two double beds, private bath, air-conditioning, color TV, and a swimming pool shared with dozens of other guests. Meanwhile, as the Outer Banks welcomes more than five million visitors each year, demand is growing for additional motel rooms. It remains to be seen whether that will lead modern entrepreneurs to fill that void.

One

THE GRAND DAMES

As increasing numbers of vacationers discovered the Outer Banks in the years following the Great Depression and World War II, larger and more elaborate accommodations were built along the coastline, appealing to guests wanting to enjoy sun and sand as well as dinner and dancing.

Mid-20th-century Outer Banks hotel amenities included private baths with hot and cold running water; large, airy porches; in-room telephones; and dining rooms with oceanfront views. Noteworthy guests included governors, ambassadors, senators, and business leaders as well as groups seeking ample room for meetings and conventions. As time progressed, many of these lodges added new features and special activities such as gift shops, swimming pools, fashion shows, and annual themed special events to attract discriminating travelers.

For years, these hotels were prominent fixtures on the Outer Banks, but most have been lost to forces of nature and travelers' changing tastes. Today, only the First Colony Inn and the Sea Ranch remain.

Severely damaged by storms and in a state of disrepair, the First Colony Inn was scheduled to be destroyed in a controlled fire in 1988 when the Nags Head Board of Commissioners passed an ordinance banning the burning of historically significant buildings. The property's new owner then offered the inn to anyone who would haul it away. Lawrence Property Management, Inc., of Lexington, North Carolina, bought the building and moved it to Milepost 16, where it reopened in 1991.

The Sea Ranch's storied history also continues. Travis and Alice Sykes opened the hotel in 1951 in the Kitty Hawk enclave of Southern Shores. Alice Sykes used her experiences working in hospitality in Virginia Beach and winters spent in California, New Mexico, and Florida to bring a new style to the Outer Banks that would capture visitors' imaginations. The Sea Ranch was billed as "strikingly different" and an "exclusive retreat." Each of its 40 rooms faced the ocean. There were weekly cocktail parties, and morning demitasse was served in guest rooms.

However, after the disastrous 1962 Ash Wednesday Storm nearly destroyed the hotel, the Sykes family rebuilt the Sea Ranch in Kill Devil Hills. Currently known as the Sea Ranch Resort, the hotel is owned and operated by dpM Partners of Gaithersburg, Maryland.

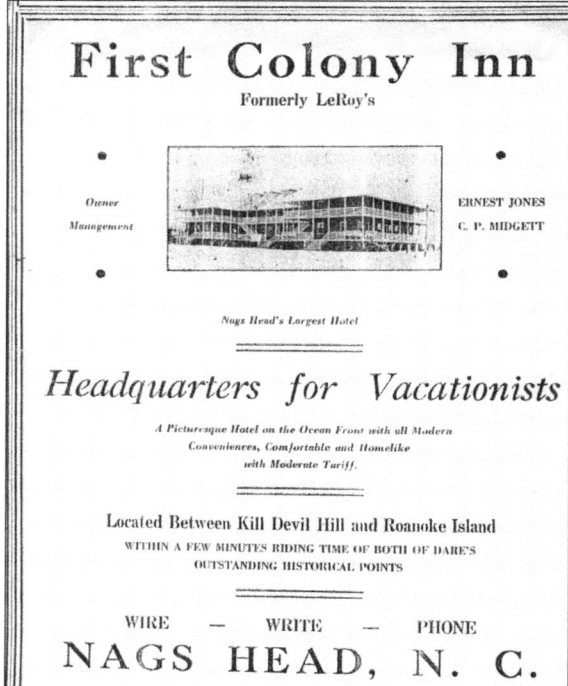

FIRST COLONY INN. After a March 1932 storm destroyed their soundside hotel, Henry and Marie LeRoy of Elizabeth City, North Carolina, opened a three-story hotel on the oceanfront across from Jockey's Ridge, naming it LeRoy's Seaside Inn. In 1937, C.P. Midgett and Ernest Jones purchased the hotel and changed its name to First Colony Inn in honor of the area's newest attraction, the outdoor drama *The Lost Colony*.

FIRST COLONY ADVERTISEMENT. By 1939, the First Colony Inn was the largest hotel on the beach. In its heyday, the inn boasted 60 rooms and a restaurant. C.P. Midgett and his wife, Daisy, purchased Ernest Jones's share of the hotel in 1940 and ran it until 1961. (Courtesy of First Colony Inn.)

THE BIG MOVE. In August 1988, the First Colony Inn was sliced into three sections and moved three and a half miles south of its original location to a 4.4-acre site at Milepost 16. After major renovations, the inn reopened in 1991 as a bed-and-breakfast. (Courtesy of First Colony Inn.)

RESTORED TO MAKE NEW MEMORIES. The First Colony Inn is a combination of Queen Anne and Colonial America architecture and features three equal sections separated by breezeways. The renovated building's 26 rooms are named in honor of 26 of the 117 colonists who established the first colony on Roanoke Island in 1587. (Courtesy of First Colony Inn.)

COMBINING THE PAST AND PRESENT. Covered in shingles representative of the beach-style architecture found throughout Nags Head in the early 20th century, the inn is the region's oldest hotel in continuous operation as a lodging establishment. In recent years, it has become a popular wedding venue. (Courtesy of First Colony Inn.)

CROATAN INN. Soon after Virginia Dare Trail was completed in the early 1930s, Russell "Skipper" and Bernie Griggs built the Croatan Inn on a section of beachfront property in what would become Kill Devil Hills. Opened in 1936 and built in stages, the inn was located directly in front of the shipwrecked *Irma*.

A STORIED HISTORY. Russell and Bernie Griggs sold the hotel to Thomas Briggs, Lorimer Midgett, and Wayne Massey of Elizabeth City, North Carolina, for $85,000 in 1954. Thomas Briggs, who had formerly operated the Fort Raleigh Hotel in Manteo, and his wife, Helen "Susie" Briggs, ran the hotel. Their son Charles Briggs became an actor, appearing in the movies *Home from the Hill* with Robert Mitchum and *Norma Rae* with Sally Field.

NEW ROAD, OLD HOTEL. The 158 Bypass had only recently been completed when this aerial photograph of the Croatan Inn was taken in July 1965. Holy Redeemer Catholic Church is pictured on the left.

COMMUNITY GATHERING PLACE. The two-story Croatan Inn was known for its clublike atmosphere, complete with a sundeck where guests gathered for social hour. The property became Papagayos Mexican Restaurant in 1981 and then Quagmires on the Beach in 1996. After falling into disrepair, the building was demolished in 2006.

THE NAGS HEADER. Forming the Nags Head Hotel Corporation, Elizabeth City businessmen Frank Dawson, W.C. Dawson, John B. McMullan, and Haywood Duke purchased 650 feet of oceanfront property—the highest acreage between Nags Head and Kitty Hawk—near Milepost 11 in Nags Head and began construction on the Nags Header in March 1935. Frank Dawson also designed the hotel, which was built at a cost of $20,000. The hotel opened on May 25, 1935. (Above, courtesy of Lara Carter.)

A NEW CHAPTER. Grayson Harding of Edenton, North Carolina, purchased the Nags Header from the Nags Head Hotel Corporation in 1943 and sold it to George C. Culpepper Sr., owner of Culpepper Motor Company in Elizabeth City, the following year. Culpepper kept a goat named Bill to trim the Nags Header's lawn, believing the animal was more efficient than a lawn mower. Bill was known to have a discriminating taste for cigarette butts, choosing to eat only Chesterfields over the variety of other brands guests tossed over the veranda. (Courtesy of Lara Carter.)

CASUAL AMBIANCE. The Nags Header featured a red shingle exterior and an expansive porch. Inside, the lobby opened onto wide verandas, and guests eating in the airy dining room enjoyed dancing to the sounds of the Nags Head Beach Club Orchestra. The kitchen included electric refrigeration. George Culpepper and his son, Clarence, who managed the hotel, both died in 1969, and their family sold the property to Elizabeth City attorney Russell Twiford in 1970. The hotel changed hands several times during the decade before it was destroyed by fire in October 1978. (Both, courtesy of Lara Carter.)

COASTAL COMFORT. In its early days, the Nags Header was billed as the "finest hotel on the Carolina coast." The three-story hotel was the first on the beach to install private baths and hot and cold running water in each of its 31 guest rooms.

THE CAROLINIAN. Opened in June 1947 at Milepost 10, the Carolinian was one of the first hotels constructed on the Outer Banks during the post–World War II building boom. It soon became known as Nags Head's most modern hotel. The brick structure included 64 rooms, all with baths and telephones, and a dining room that overlooked the ocean. Lucille Sermons Purser, her brother Wayland Sermons, and her sister and brother-in-law Lima and Julian Oneto were among a group of backers who developed the Carolinian. Purser and the Onetos ran the hotel until 1969. (Author's collection.)

OFF-SEASON ACTIVITIES. Carolinian managing owner Lucille Sermons Purser wanted to encourage business during the off season, so the Valentine's Day Fox Hunt was launched in 1949 and continued annually into the early 1970s. Instead of horses, jeeps and stock cars were used in the hunt, which took place on Bodie Island, Colington Island, and in Nags Head Woods. By the mid-1950s, the fox hunt had gained national attention, often attracting 100 hunters.

SPECIAL EVENTS. The Carolinian also regularly hosted fashion and art shows, Sea Hags fishing tournaments, jeep races on Jockey's Ridge, and kite-flying competitions. Julian Oneto, the hotel's resident manager, was elected Nags Head's first mayor in 1961. Known for his Hatteras-style clam chowder, Oneto also played the guitar and led singalongs during beach bonfires in front of the Carolinian.

PIRATES JAMBOREE. Along with other local businesses, the Carolinian developed the Dare Coast Pirates Jamboree in the early 1950s. The annual spring festival launched the tourist season on the Outer Banks with parades, dances, costume contests, fish fries, boat races, beach buggy races, mock pirate battles, and other events in Kitty Hawk, Kill Devil Hills, Nags Head, Roanoke Island, and Hatteras. What began as a three-day event expanded to weeklong festivities and finally to the four-week long Jamborama in 1963. The last Pirates Jamboree was held in 1964 amid concerns that ever-increasing crowds strained the area's limited resources.

PIRATE ROYALTY. In 1959, Carolinian owner-manager Julian Oneto and Winona Gray were crowned king and queen of the Pirates Jamboree during the Grand Pirates Ball. To compete for the royal crown, Oneto and many other local men began growing beards months before the Jamboree.

SEASIDE ELEGANCE. In 1953, a solarium and 24 units were added to the Carolinian, and its dining room was enlarged. By 1964, it was the largest hotel on the Outer Banks. Guests during the hotel's early days dressed for dinner and were assigned the same waiter each night. In 1959, Miss North Carolina Betty Lane Evans dedicated the hotel's new pool during festivities that included a poolside fashion show.

A STURDY STRUCTURE. Long considered to be the strongest building on the beach, the Carolinian served as the hurricane headquarters for media members who flocked to the Outer Banks when severe storms approached. The hotel even withstood the powerful Ash Wednesday Storm in March 1962, which resulted in severe flooding. Still, despite its grand history, the Carolinian fell into despair and was demolished in April 2001.

SEA RANCH. Travis and Alice Sykes of Virginia Beach, Virginia, built the original Sea Ranch in Southern Shores in 1951. At the time, the 40-room lodge was the Outer Banks' most northern hotel. After the building was ravaged by the 1962 Ash Wednesday Storm, the couple rebuilt in Kill Devil Hills, opening the current Sea Ranch in June 1963.

OUTER BANKS HIGH-RISE. In December 1967, ground was broken on the Sea Ranch's five-story addition, the first high-rise on the Outer Banks. The hotel expanded to 104 units in 1968.

OUTER BANKS ORIGINAL. Over the years, the Sea Ranch became known for other firsts, including the Outer Banks' first indoor heated pool installed in 1973 and the area's first indoor tennis facility, opened in 1979. dpM Partners purchased the hotel in two phases beginning in 2010 and launched extensive renovations in 2011.

THE ARLINGTON HOTEL. The inn was known as Modlin's Hotel when it was built on the Nags Head soundside in the early 1900s. It was relocated to the oceanfront near Milepost 14 after the construction of Virginia Dare Trail. For many years, the Arlington was the first Nags Head hotel visitors saw when approaching from the south.

GRACIOUS HOSPITALITY. Dewey and Phoebe Hayman bought the Arlington in 1944. Under the Haymans' leadership, the hotel was listed in Duncan Hines's 1948 Vacation Guide. The couple also opened the Seafare Oyster Bar across from the hotel in 1959. Dewey Hayman served as mayor of Nags Head and a delegate in the North Carolina General Assembly, where he was instrumental in forming the Cape Hatteras National Seashore Commission.

BEACHFRONT EXPANSION. The Haymans added a new wing to the hotel in 1950 and expanded it again in 1954 with a larger dining room, lobby, lounge, verandas, and recreational facilities. The Arlington was one of the few buildings on the beach that had a basement. It was used for employee quarters, a walk-in refrigerator, a hot-water boiler, and a storeroom. (Courtesy of Pam Gladden.)

DEVASTATING LOSS. The Arlington survived the 1962 Ash Wednesday Storm, although its dining room was swept out to sea. However, the fury of a February 1973 nor'easter proved too much for the venerable hotel. It was destroyed when its center section fell into the ocean during the storm. At the time, the Arlington was Nags Head's oldest business. (Courtesy of April Ross.)

Two

NAGS HEAD

Nags Head holds the distinction as North Carolina's oldest coastal summer resort, welcoming vacationers as early as the 1750s. Unlike other coastal areas, Nags Head remained untouched by commercial and industrial development in the 18th and 19th centuries. When development did take place, it mainly occurred on the soundside, where wealthy residents from the mainland built summer cottages for their families. When people began moving closer to the beach in the early 1900s, they built simple wood-frame cottages and later hotels on the oceanfront. Nags Head's popularity as a vacation spot continued to grow throughout the 20th century, with hotels, motels, and cottage courts lining the coastline, each with a unique design and qualities.

NAG'S HEAD HOTEL.

This delightful Summer Resort will be open for the reception of visitors on the

25th Day of June, 1890.

The charge for Board will be as follows:

Per day,	$2.00
Per week,	10.00
Per month, 1 room occupied exclusively by one person,	50.00
Per month, 1 room occupied exclusively by two persons,	35.00
Per month, 1 room occupied exclusively by three persons,	30.00

Special Rates to Families of Four or More Persons.

Apply to the undersigned early for select rooms. Reserved rooms will be charged for from **June 25th**.

The buildings are new and comfortably arranged; furniture also new. The table will be the best, and servants attentive.

— **Daily Steamer**. —

J. M. WHEDBEE,
Manager,

NAG'S HEAD HOTEL. This advertisement from the May 20, 1890, issue of the Elizabeth City *Weekly Economist* promoted one of Nags Head's first hotels, a soundside business that offered guests a variety of activities during the summer including train rides from the hotel to the oceanfront.

Sea Oatel. Manteo merchant Archie Burrus and his wife, Lina, built this 20-room motel in 1953 near Milepost 16. Consisting of four brick-veneer buildings, the motel featured all-tile bathrooms. A pool and a restaurant, the Darolina, were added in 1959. Over the years, the Sea Oatel expanded several times to eventually include 119 units. (Above, author's collection.)

OUTER BANKS QUALITY INN. One of the first elevators on the Outer Banks was installed in the Sea Oatel in 1968. Damaged during 2003's Hurricane Isabel, the motel was demolished in 2005. It had been in operation for approximately 40 years.

SEA FOAM MOTEL. Opened in 1948, the one-story brick motel was one of the first on the beach to have an inground swimming pool. Original owners Theodore and Rosa Meekins both died in 1954, and their sons, Theodore S. Meekins Jr. and Percy W. Meekins, inherited the property. Theodore and his wife, Goldie H. Meekins, continued to operate the motel until it was sold in 1976. Lee and Kitty Raver of Richmond, Virginia, have owned the Sea Foam since 1989. (Author's collection.)

OCEANFRONT EXPANSION. A two-story wing facing the ocean was added to the Sea Foam in 1951. A section of the motel's two-story north wing was built in the mid-1950s, and the three wings were connected at the corners. A two-story extension was added to the north wing in 1964.

HISTORIC ACCOMMODATIONS. The 51-unit Sea Foam has been listed in the National Register of Historic Places since 2004. Many of the motel's older guest rooms retain their original knotty-pine paneling as well as the original bathroom fixtures.

A Dream Realized. Ahoskie, North Carolina, native Marvin Minton had always wanted to open a motel in Nags Head, saying that Outer Banks people were among the friendliest he had ever met. Minton and his wife, Hazel, a Kitty Hawk native, opened the Beachcomber in 1959. In a 1967 article in the *Coastland Times*, Minton was quoted as saying, "The nice thing about most vacationers is that they're just that. Vacationing. They're relaxed, happy to talk, pleasant and seem genuinely grateful for good service and a little extra attention." (Below, courtesy of Rodney Minton.)

BEACHCOMBER HOTEL. The Beachcomber was enlarged in the early 1960s to 22 units. It was later razed and replaced by large cottages. (Courtesy of Rodney Minton.)

THE VACATIONER MOTEL. For more than a decade, Robert E. Ownley, an electrical engineering professor at the West Virginia Institute of Technology, rented out his four-bedroom cottage at the base of Jockey's Ridge. In the early 1960s, Ownley purchased property at Milepost 16, where he moved the cottage, purchased two other cottages, and built a motel with 12 rooms and efficiencies. The Vacationer opened on the birthday of his wife, Ann, in June 1964. (Author's collection.)

SUCCESSFUL BUSINESS. Like many other motels on the Outer Banks, The Vacationer enjoyed brisk business from the time it opened, allowing owners Bob and Ann Ownley to pay off their mortgage in five years. In 1972, the Ownleys sold the pink oceanfront cottage and built a three-story building containing 11 rooms and efficiencies and a two-room apartment. (Below, author's collection.)

ROOMS — EFFICIENCIES — COTTAGES — APARTMENTS

The
Vacationer
MOTEL
THE 16 MILE POST -:- "ON THE OCEAN"
NAGS HEAD, N. C. 27959
TEL. 919-441-7487
BOB, ANN and BETH OWNLEY, Proprietors
JIMMY and HOPE OWNLEY, Managers
POOL — AIR CONDITIONED — T.V. — ELECTRIC HEAT

WESTSIDE EXPANSION. The Vacationer also included two two-room apartments on the west side of Virginia Dare Trail across from the motel. The apartments were rebuilt following a 1982 Palm Sunday brush fire that began on the soundside and was carried across the bypass by strong wind gusts. That building is all that remains of The Vacationer after it was sold and demolished in 2000. (Author's collection.)

NAGS HEAD LANDMARK. Arriving on the Outer Banks in the early 1950s, entrepreneur George Crocker Jr. borrowed $15,000 to build the Beacon Motor Lodge. Over the next two decades, he purchased a small sportswear shop across the street from the Beacon that he expanded to become the Galleon Esplanade, and he built another motel, the Cabana East, and A Restaurant by George. Crocker had sold his interests in these businesses before he died in 1998.

CABANA EAST. The 32-unit motel was under construction in the late winter of 1962 when the Ash Wednesday Storm ravaged its foundation. However, the motel's principal stockholder, George Crocker Jr., oversaw repairs and ensured that construction was completed in time for the 1962 summer season. The motel was sold to developers in the late 1990s and torn down. (Author's collection.)

BEACON MOTOR LODGE. Opened in the spring of 1955, the Beacon was developed by George C. Crocker and Associates of Norfolk, Virginia. The white-and-blue motel featured an oceanfront dining room, high-fidelity music piped to all guest rooms and public places, and dancing to live music on the patio. Closed at the end of the 2013 season, the Beacon was demolished in 2015. (Below, courtesy of Pam Gladden.)

FIN 'N FEATHER MOTEL. Dare County natives Willett and Jeanine Tillett opened the blue ceramic brick motel on the Nags Head–Manteo causeway in the summer of 1967. It quickly became a favorite of fishermen and hunters. The motel closed after it was damaged during Hurricane Irene in 2011. Local developer Jim Rose later bought and refurbished it. The motel is now known as the Fin N' Feather Waterside Inn.

HOTEL PARKERSON. Leven and Elizabeth Parkerson built their namesake hotel near Milepost 10 in 1936. After her husband was electrocuted during a storm in 1944, Elizabeth Parkerson continued to run the hotel until selling it in 1960. A problem with the transaction led the sale to be tied up in court, during which time the hotel was damaged by fire and by the 1962 Ash Wednesday Storm.

COMFORTABLE ROOMS, GOOD FOOD. Known for its hospitality and fine food, the Hotel Parkerson served fresh fish caught in nets 300 yards from the hotel. Other specialties included deviled clams, Southern fried chicken, and owner Elizabeth Parkerson's homemade pies. (Author's collection.)

SHORE ACRE MOTEL. George and Mary Spencer of Columbia, North Carolina, opened the pastel-shaded motel near Milepost 16 in the late 1940s. After her husband's death in 1953, Mary Spencer continued to run the motel until selling it in 1973.

UNIQUE DESIGN. Horace and Vivian Parker opened the Vivianna near Milepost 16 in 1961. With a roof over each of its nine units, the gray stone structure brought a distinctive new look to Nags Head motels. The architectural design also featured a glass-front lounge and office located in the center of the motel.

The Vivianna. Newport News, Virginia, physician Sarah Forbes purchased the motel in 1997. She sold the land in 2000, intending to move the motel to a nearby site. However, the Vivianna was torn down after Forbes was unable to submit a site plan to the Nags Head Board of Commissioners within the allotted timeframe. (Courtesy of Pam Gladden.)

Sandpebble Efficiencies. These efficiencies and apartments opened at Milepost 12 in 1969 as Sheryl Efficiencies, named for the daughter of owners George and Mary Ansell. The couple sold the property later that year to Lon Edwards, who changed the name to Sandpebble Efficiency Apartments. George Ansell returned as manager in 1982, staying until the property was sold and demolished in 2001. It was replaced with luxury homes.

PEBBLE BEACH MOTEL. This motel was restored after sustaining heavy damage during the 1962 Ash Wednesday Storm. In 1966, the adjacent Jewart's Cottages became part of the motel when James and Mildred Jewart sold the units to Pebble Beach owners Roy Wicker and Edward A. Coyner Jr. The Pebble Beach was torn down in early 2002.

THE NAGS HEAD INN. Frank and Donis White, along with Dare County sheriff Frank Cahoon and his wife, Charlotte, and W.W. Tarkington, opened the Miramar in 1951. Adjacent to St. Andrew's Episcopal Church and across the street from the Arlington Hotel, the tourist court became the Nags Head Inn after it was sold in the early 1960s. The structure was destroyed during a controlled burn by the Nags Head Fire Department in 1986.

EVANS COTTAGES AND APARTMENTS. Evelyn Evans operated the lodging establishment near Milepost 16. The property was torn down in 2003.

HOWELL'S COTTAGES. W.O. "Willie" Howell had Howell's Cottages built in 1951 and operated the property until 1957, when he sold it to Alabama native Jewell Graves.

THE SAND DOLLAR. After purchasing Howell's Cottages in Nags Head in 1957, Jewell Graves renamed it the Sand Dollar. She also expanded the property to include two two-story oceanfront buildings and a second-floor addition to the building facing the highway. Graves had a long association with the American Red Cross and often assisted local Red Cross teams after hurricanes and other natural disasters.

SEAPORT FISHING PIER AND OUTER BANKS FISHING PIER. A.E. "Red" and Bertha Mitchell owned the Seaport Fishing Pier in South Nags Head, which included three cottages and a duplex. Robert W. Oliver and his son, Garry Oliver, bought the pier complex in 1970, renaming it the Outer Banks Fishing Pier.

JEANETTE'S MOTOR COURT AND OCEAN PIER. When Warren H. Jennette Sr. opened Jennette's Fishing Pier at Whalebone Junction in 1939, the business included a restaurant and cottages that had previously housed some of the 1,500 US Civil Works Administration workers who built protective sand dunes along the Outer Banks in the early 1930s. Over the years, the pier sustained damage from various storms, culminating in the loss of about 540 feet of the structure during Hurricane Isabel in 2003. The new owner, the North Carolina Aquarium Society, rebuilt it as a 1,000-foot-long educational ocean pier. The new $25 million Jennette's Pier opened in 2011 as part of the Aquariums Division of the North Carolina Department of Environment and Natural Resources.

DOLPHIN MOTOR COURT. Located south of Jennette's Fishing Pier, the Dolphin Motor Court was the closest motel to the Cape Hatteras National Seashore when it was completed in the summer of 1952. Within a few weeks of the motel's completion, owner Fearings, Inc., sold it to Bertha Sample of Elizabeth City for $100,000. The following year, Sample converted the motel's office into a breakfast room, setting up three tables to serve guests a morning meal.

AN OUTER BANKS FIXTURE. As it approaches its 70th year in business, the Dolphin continues to be a Nags Head landmark. The 45-room lodge was renovated in 2017 and is now known as the Dolphin Oceanfront Motel.

ISLANDER MOTEL. Edward Thompson achieved his dream of owning a motel on the Outer Banks when he opened the Islander near Milepost 16 in 1973. Thompson's wife, Sylvia, dug up cacti and sandspurs on the property because she wanted children to be able to run around barefoot without getting stuck. She also planted trees around the motel for shade. Pictured are Edward and Sylvia Thompson. (Courtesy of Elizabeth Thompson Seawell.)

SPECIAL GUEST. Lady Bird Johnson, the widow of former president Lyndon B. Johnson, was a guest at the Islander in 1978 when she visited her niece who lived in Manteo. Mrs. Johnson brought with her six Secret Service agents, including a sniper who was positioned on the motel's roof. According to Elizabeth Thompson Seawell, the Thompsons' daughter and current owner of the Islander, Mrs. Johnson wanted a daiquiri, but local laws prohibited restaurants from selling liquor by the drink. Edward Thompson offered to make her a daiquiri, but in his excitement, he accidently gave her a double portion. The next morning, the former first lady declared it was the best daiquiri she had ever had. Pictured on the Islander grounds are, from left to right, Lady Bird Johnson, Edward Thompson, Sylvia Thompson, and Elizabeth Thompson. (Courtesy of Elizabeth Thompson Seawell.)

HOSTING A BIG CATCH. A guest staying at the Islander caught a record blue marlin aboard a chartered boat out of Oregon Inlet in 1974. The fish topped the scales at 1,142 pounds, a world record that stood until 1986. The guest called Islander owner Edward Thompson from a ship-to-shore telephone, and Thompson, along with his daughter, hurried to the Oregon Inlet Fishing Center to meet the boat when it arrived with its massive catch. (Courtesy of Elizabeth Thompson Seawell.)

SILVER SANDS. Dare County natives Jule Burrus and his sister Estelle Tillett opened this motel at Milepost 14 in the mid-1950s. At the time, it was one of the few new motels built opposite the ocean side. The Silver Sands was torn down in 2002.

BLUE WATERS MOTOR COURT. The Reverend LeRoy Leppard and his wife, Ruby, moved to Nags Head from South Carolina in 1958 and opened the Blue Waters Motor Court. After her husband died in 1965, Ruby continued to run the cottage court until she sold it in 1983. The cottages were demolished in the 1990s.

A.E. SADLER COTTAGES. A.E. Sadler opened the cottage court bearing his name in 1961. Located on the oceanfront across from Jockey's Ridge, the property was advertised as "two- and three-bedroom cottages, not a motor court." Each of the 15 cottages featured "Hollywood-type beds with the best box springs and mattresses." Sadler's son and daughter-in-law, Edward L. "Budgie" and Anna Daniels Sadler, ran the court from 1968 through 1980. The property was sold in 1985, and the cottages were later relocated to sites in Kill Devil Hills and on Roanoke Island.

OCEAN HOUSE. The Ocean House became the first truly brick motel on the beach when Frank Cahoon, W.W. Tarkington, and Frank and Donis White opened the 20-unit lodge in 1955. Over the years, the motel expanded to 42 rooms. Tanya Young purchased the property in 1979, renamed it Tanya's Ocean House, and renovated its rooms using themes such as Nags Head Woods, Blackbeard's Watering Hole, and the Pioneer Room. Several large beach houses replaced the motel after it was torn down in 2012. (Author's collection.)

OWENS' MOTEL. Robert and Clara Owens opened a tourist court and café near Whalebone Junction in 1946. After her husband's sudden death in 1950, Clara Owens continued to run the business, serving three meals a day starting with breakfast at dawn. Originally known as Owens' Tourist Court, the motel and restaurant are still run by the Owenses' daughter Clara Mae Shannon and her family. Owens' Restaurant is the oldest restaurant in North Carolina run by the same family at the same location. The motel includes oceanside rooms and efficiencies, an apartment, a westside courtyard, and westside rooms. (Above, author's collection.)

SEA SPRAY TOURIST HOME. The Sea Spray began as a tourist home on the west side of the beach road in 1941. William F. "Bug" Tillett, a Manns Harbor shrimper and boat builder, constructed the establishment, and his adopted son and daughter-in-law, Richard and Lessie Mann, assisted in managing the old-style bed-and-breakfast. In 1952, the Manns opened the six-unit Sea Spray Cottage Court on the oceanfront across from the Sea Spray Tourist Home. (Above, painting by Louise Riley, courtesy of Cyndy Mann Holda; below, courtesy of Cyndy Mann Holda.)

SEA SPRAY MOTEL. Richard and Lessie Mann, owners of the Sea Spray Cottage Court, and business partners Willis and Elizabeth Jessup of Hertford, North Carolina, built the six-unit Sea Spray Motel on oceanfront land they purchased south of the Nags Head Fishing Pier. The Manns later bought the Jessups' share of the motel and expanded it to 24 units. During the off-season, their youngest daughter, Cyndy, kept her horse in a stable at the motel. The Manns ran the Sea Spray until selling the property in the early 1980s. The motel sat empty for several years before it was torn down in late 2006.

ATLANTIC VIEW COTTAGES. William F. "Bug" Tillett and his wife, Mattie, built the Atlantic View as a tourist home on the west side of Virginia Dare Trail. Later, after the Atlantic View was sold, Jaccie Burrus, whom the Tilletts had raised, built four cottages across from the property, naming them Atlantic View Cottages. Burrus and his wife, Thelma, owned and operated the cottages for more than 30 years. Under new ownership, the cottage court has been renamed 2 Fish Cay.

SUN LUCK COTTAGES. These oceanfront units adjacent to the Atlantic View Cottages were originally known as the Sea Spray Cottage Court. After Richard and Lessie Mann sold the property in 1964, the new owners expanded it and changed the name to Sun Luck Cottages.

LONDON INN. Hotel developer John Yancey opened the 48-unit London Inn at Milepost 12 in 1969. Later known as the Olde London Inn, the motel was demolished in 2001.

HOLLOWELL'S HOTEL. Pasquotank County native Graham Hollowell built a combination hotel and store on the Roanoke Sound near Jockey's Ridge in 1910. Hollowell's enterprise included a pier where passengers arriving via steamer disembarked. After a March 1933 storm, Hollowell moved the building to the ocean side by rolling it on logs. The property was also the site of the Nags Head Post Office from 1928 to 1946. Hollowell and his wife, Ethel, kept horses and cows in the field adjacent to the hotel and store until the animals drowned during the 1962 Ash Wednesday Storm. The building has since been demolished.

COLONIAL INN. Lionel and Plum Edwards opened the Colonial Inn and Tourist Court next to the new Mann's Ocean Pier (forerunner of the Nags Head Fishing Pier) in 1947. The couple was instrumental in founding the town of Nags Head and its volunteer fire department. Robert Norris purchased the Colonial Inn in the 1960s and ran it until 1997. His daughter and son-in-law, Carolyn and Everett Fifield, then owned and operated the motel until 2007. Renovated in 2019, the motel is currently owned by MKL Hospitality Management Group. (Both, courtesy of the Colonial Inn.)

COLONIAL INN RESTAURANT. The Colonial Inn's restaurant was known for its fried chicken, hamburger steak, and lamb chops. It was torn down in the early 1970s to make room for the motel's swimming pool. (Above, courtesy of the Colonial Inn; below, courtesy of April Ross.)

SURFSIDE HOTEL. Opened in 1984 near Milepost 16, the Surfside Hotel includes 76 rooms and indoor and outdoor pools. (Courtesy of Pam Gladden.)

EL GAY MOTOR COURT. Brothers Edward L. and Elmer E. Brown opened the 10-unit El Gay Motor Court between Mileposts 15 and 16 in Nags Head in 1952. The motel was named for Edward Brown's children, Edward Lee Jr. and Gayle. The following year, they converted the adjacent house into the El Gay Restaurant, because Edward Brown was convinced that more people would visit Nags Head during the winter if they were able to find a restaurant open for business.

MANOR MOTEL. By the late 1960s, the El Gay Motor Court had become the Gay Manor. In later years, it was known as the Manor Motel. David and Maryann Maryott of Bethesda, Maryland, pictured below, purchased the business in 1990. At that time, there were 17 units and two cottages. The Maryotts sold the motel in 2004 but continued to manage it for another year until it was sold again. The Manor Motel was torn down in 2010 and replaced by large houses. (Both, courtesy of David and Maryann Maryott.)

CAHOON'S MARKET AND COTTAGES. Ray V. and Dorothy Cahoon and Ray's brother, Charlie Cahoon, purchased Evans Place in 1962, transforming it into Cahoon's Variety/Market and Cottages. The cottages include 10 two-, three-, and four-bedroom cottages and two efficiency units.

SANDSPUR. Samuel and Nancy Burrus opened this cottage court between Mileposts 15 and 16 in 1959. The 21-unit property has passed through several owners over the years and underwent extensive renovations after local developer Jim Rose purchased it in 2015.

WHITE MARLIN MOTOR COURT. Opened in the mid-1960s just south of Whalebone Junction, these modular efficiency units were dismantled and moved in the early 1980s.

OCEANSIDE COURT. Located between Mileposts 15 and 16, the cottage court has been a Nags Head fixture for more than 50 years. It is now managed by KEES Vacations.

GREGORY'S COTTAGES AND OCEAN VERANDA. Sanford and Marjorie Gregory owned a cottage court and general store near the Nags Head–Kill Devil Hills line for more than two decades. They sold the property in 1972. Next door, the Ocean Veranda was razed in 2002.

WHALEBONE MOTEL. Located at Milepost 17, the 1960s-era motel lost an oceanfront section of rooms during Hurricane Isabel in 2003. Local developer Jim Rose later purchased the motel and initially planned to renovate it. Realizing that would not be feasible, Rose decided to tear down the motel and replace it with seven cottages similar to ones that populated the Outer Banks during the 1950s and 1960s. Opened in 2018, Whalebone Cottage Court is Nags Head's first new cottage court in about 40 years.

BLUE HERON. Owned by Wilma Gladden and her family since 1969, this motel at Milepost 16 opened in 1965 with 12 units in a two-story building. The Gladdens have expanded the motel several times over the years, including adding a three-story south building in 1984–1985 and a third floor to the original building. Every room in the motel faces the ocean. (Both, courtesy of Pam Gladden.)

NAGS HEAD MAINSTAY. The Blue Heron's south building has 12 units, as well as an indoor heated pool and hot tub. There is also an oceanfront outdoor pool. Although the property has been listed for sale, the Gladden family continues to welcome guests, many of whom have made annual visits to the motel for decades. (Both, courtesy of Pam Gladden.)

BRICK'S SERVICE STATION AND COTTAGES. Commercial fisherman Clarence "Brick" Brickle and his wife, Dorothy, purchased the property between Mileposts 15 and 16 in 1961. Brickle, who served as Nags Head mayor in the late 1960s and early 1970s, at one time kept the town's only fire truck on his property. After Brickle's death in 1972, his widow continued to run the business until 1984. It was razed in 2014 after sitting empty for several years.

TAR HEEL MOTEL. George and Anne Corey of Williamston, North Carolina, bought the Star Motel near Milepost 16 in 1961 and refurbished it as the Tar Heel Motel. The Outer Banks Hotel Group purchased the motel in 2018. The group—investors seeking to preserve older motels—renovated the Tar Heel, naming its 32 updated rooms after fish and local bodies of water. The Tar Heel reopened in time for the 2018 summer season.

Three
KILL DEVIL HILLS

Today, Kill Devil Hills is the Outer Banks' most populous community with about 6,800 year-round residents, a significant feat for a town that was not incorporated until 1953. By that time, several hotels and motels had already sprung up, luring travelers by their proximity not only to the ocean but also to the Wright Brothers Memorial, celebrating man's first successful powered flight. Motels continued to be added to the town's landscape throughout the 1960s and 1970s. The town is now home to nearly 20 motels and hotels, about half of which are national chains.

WILBUR WRIGHT HOTEL. Capt. Thomas A. Baum, who ran the first scheduled ferry from Kitty Hawk to Point Harbor in Currituck County, built this three-story, 47-room hotel in 1939 at a cost of more than $20,000. At the time, the Wilbur Wright was the third largest hotel on the beach. This photograph was taken in 1940.

WRIGHT CONNECTION. Preparing to open his new hotel, Capt. Thomas A. Baum asked Orville Wright if he could name the establishment in his honor. Wright declined the honor, requesting that Baum name the hotel for his brother, Wilbur, who had died in 1912. However, Orville Wright added that if Baum ever built another hotel, he could name that one after him. (Author's collection.)

FULL SERVICE HOTEL. The Wilbur Wright Hotel included the First Flight Room restaurant, which served more than 1,000 meals during the summer season, and the Fly High Room lounge. One year before the 40th anniversary of its opening, the hotel was destroyed by a waterspout in July 1978.

ORVILLE WRIGHT MOTOR LODGE. Thomas Baum's daughter, Diane Baum St. Clair, built the Orville Wright Motor Lodge adjacent to the Wilbur Wright Hotel in 1948. After the Wilbur Wright Hotel was destroyed by a waterspout in 1978, St. Clair renamed the Orville Wright the Wilbur and Orville Wright Motor Lodge. Now known as the Days Inn Oceanfront Wright Brothers, the lodge is the Outer Banks' longest continuously running hotel.

KITTY HAWK MOTOR LODGE. Edmund and Goldie Melson of Newport News, Virginia, opened the Hotel Kitty Hawk in 1946. The lodge's dining room featured fresh seafood from Colington fishermen. After undergoing extensive renovations in 1968, including the addition of apartments and cottages, the property was renamed the Kitty Hawk Motor Lodge. Edmund Melson also served as a Kill Devil Hills commissioner.

CAVALIER MOTOR COURT. Manteo Furniture owner Roy Wescott Sr. opened this motel on Memorial Day weekend 1950. Wescott had purchased the property from local realtor Theodore Meekins for $9,000, sealing the deal with a handshake. The next day, another man offered Meekins $10,000 for the property, but he refused, saying, "I can't do it. I shook hands with Roy Wescott yesterday." Wescott's daughter, Dale Wescott, credits the motel's longevity to its repeat customers. Many guests return each year, including some who have annually stayed at the Cavalier for more than 50 years. (Courtesy of Dale Wescott.)

FIRST OUTER BANKS MOTOR COURT. The Cavalier Motor Court was the first Outer Banks motel built in the motor court style, in which vehicles entered on one side of the property and exited on the other. The motel, which has always stayed open year-round, initially had 19 separate flat-roofed units. Today, there are 54 units. (Courtesy of Dale Wescott.)

Dive In. Initially, Roy and Dorothy Wescott and Herman and Alice Minges of Lumberton, North Carolina, jointly owned the Cavalier, but the Wescotts later bought out the other couple's share of the motel. In 1955, the Cavalier became the second motel on the Outer Banks to install a swimming pool. Two pools—one for adults and one for children—were built in the center of the property. Cavalier owner Dale Wescott recalled one guest telling her that over the years, he, his children, and his grandchildren all learned to swim in the Cavalier pool. (Both, courtesy of Dale Wescott.)

CAVALIER BY THE SEA. Cavalier owner Roy Wescott Sr. selected the motel's name from a dog racetrack near Virginia Beach. The motel is now known as The Cavalier By The Sea. Wescott, who died in 2007 at the age of 93, maintained a strong work ethic throughout his life, even going into his office at Manteo Furniture daily until the day before his death. (Courtesy of Dale Wescott.)

VIRGINIA DARE RESTAURANT AND MOTEL. This establishment was located on the Nags Head–Kill Devil Hills line. One of the oldest on the beach, the restaurant later housed Ship's Wheel, and the lodge became the Ebb Tide Motel. The building was demolished in 2015.

JOHN YANCEY MOTEL. Opened in 1962, this motel was one of the first properties developed by the John Yancey Company of Norfolk, Virginia, which owned 15 hotels and motels at its peak. Located at Milepost 10, the 40-unit motel featured telephones in every room. A second building was added in the 1970s, with more additions in the early 1980s. The property was one of the company's last motels to be sold.

JOHN YANCEY OCEANFRONT INN. Along with a name change, the motel has undergone several renovations over the years, including complete overhauls of the Sea Building in 2013 and the Four Seasons Building in 2019. It currently has 108 rooms. (Author's collection.)

OUTER BANKS MOTOR LODGE. John M. Bell, owner of the Nags Head Supermarket, opened the 18-unit Outer Banks Motor Lodge in 1961. Fifteen more units were added in 1964, along with the Driftwood Key Club, a meeting and convention venue that could accommodate up to 225 people.

SWIMMING POOL FUN. As a teenager, Eddie Miller worked as a pool boy at the Outer Banks Motor Lodge. In 1988, Miller and his wife, Lou, purchased the motel. They sold it in 2002, but they and their daughter Alexandra repurchased the property in 2012. (Courtesy of Alexandra Miller Saunders.)

MOTEL MANAGER. Vance Ross was the manager of the Outer Banks Motor Lodge in the 1970s and 1980s. Ross previously managed the Colonial Inn in Nags Head. (Courtesy of Alexandra Miller Saunders.)

BEL-AIR MOTEL. Opened in 1960, the oceanfront Bel-Air Motel advertised rooms with baths, cottages on private lots, and housekeeping apartments with screened porches. In 1963, a harbor seal found in waters off the Outer Banks was temporarily kept in the Bel-Air's swimming pool until it could be transported to a veterinarian in Chapel Hill, North Carolina. The motel was torn down in 1992 after suffering heavy damage during a 1991 Halloween storm.

THE CHART HOUSE. George "Bill" and Bettye Jones opened the Chart House Motel in 1966 and owned it for nearly 20 years. The motel has since been replaced by large cottages.

CLAYDON MOTOR LODGE. William C. and Betty Morrisette purchased Townley's Motel in the 1960s and renamed it ClayDon Motor Lodge after their sons, Clay and Don. Located between Mileposts 6 and 7, the lodge was bulldozed in early 1990 after a nor'easter the previous year destroyed one of the cottages on the property and eroded the foundation of the main building.

COLONY IV LODGE. Brothers Ralph and Briggs Neal opened the Colony IV Motel in 1971. The Neal family sold the motel in 2004. Following extensive renovations, the motel is now known as Shutters on the Banks.

TAN-A-RAMA MOTEL. Robert Young, owner of Robert A. Young and Associates, Inc., opened the Tan-A-Rama Motel next to the Avalon Pier in Kill Devil Hills in 1963. The motel was damaged during Hurricane Isabel in 2003 and later razed.

THE SUN 'N SAND MOTEL. Clayton Tillett opened this motel in the early 1950s. The Sun 'n Sand advertised connecting rooms, efficiency apartments, and private baths, and guests could park directly in front of their rooms.

THE CHEROKEE INN. Walter and Ruby Drinkwater Perry opened this fishing and hunting lodge at Milepost 8 in 1946. It is now operated as a five-room bed-and-breakfast called Cypress House Inn.

NETTLEWOOD MOTEL. Located at Milepost 7, the Nettlewood Motel was demolished after Hurricane Isabel struck the Outer Banks in 2003.

THE MARINER MOTEL. Opened in the 1960s next to the Sea Ranch, the Mariner has withstood the Atlantic Ocean's fury over the years, including battering from a 1989 winter storm that washed away part of the motel's swimming pool. Part of the Days Inn brand since the early 1990s, the motel is operated as a Days Inn and Suites by Wyndham.

TANGLEWOOD MOTEL. The Tanglewood started out as a motel when it opened in the early 1950s at Milepost 8. Its name was later changed to Tanglewood Inn. The property was razed in the early 2000s.

SEE SEA MOTEL. John C. Peterson built this motel on the west side of the Beach Road in the early 1950s. The Outer Banks Hotel Group purchased the See Sea in 2018 and refurbished each of its 23 rooms and suites with decor appealing to surfers and younger vacationers.

KILL DEVIL MANOR. Hit hard by various storms over the years, this motel was condemned after an October 1983 nor'easter knocked out its septic system and damaged four of its 12 units. A wooden bulkhead, built to shore up the motel's foundation, extended its life for several years, but the structure was eventually torn down in 1990.

Nags Lantern Cottages. Washington, DC, architect Donald Olivola designed and owned these unique cottages, which were replaced in the early 1980s by the Outer Banks Beach Club. Olivola was also the architect for Holy Redeemer Church by the Sea in Kill Devil Hills.

OCEAN VIEW COTTAGE COURT. The cottage court opened next to the Kitty Hawk Hotel in 1951. It was enlarged several times over the years, including the addition of two three-bedroom apartments, six two-bedroom efficiencies, and a swimming pool in 1968. Owners through the years included P.L. Powell, Charles and Lynn Bailey, and Alvan and Christine Hatch, who acquired the property in 1973.

THE CAT'S MEOW. Sarah Halliburton, a former correspondent for the *Raleigh News & Observer*, owned a group of cottages in the 1950s and early 1960s that she named the Cat's Meow. Halliburton, who wrote a regular column for the *Coastland Times*, died in 1965.

THE FANTASY MOTOR LODGE. Dare County attorneys Wallace H. and Sue Vick McCown owned this motel in the 1970s.

ANCHORAGE MOTEL AND APARTMENTS. William and Mildred Perry Foreman purchased this business at Milepost 9 in 1962 and named it Foreman's. They added a strip of motel rooms and a gift shop and moved the restaurant, the Pirate's Den, to the northeast corner of the property. Steve and Karen Sawin bought the establishment in 1972 and renamed it the Anchorage Motel and Apartments. Karen Sawin later converted the gift shop into the beach's first thrift store, the Merry Go Round. After the Sawins retired in 2004, they sold two of the three lots where the business was located. The buildings, except for the Pirate's Den and the owners' home, which William Foreman built, were demolished and replaced with large cottages. (Courtesy of Susan Sawin.)

Four

KITTY HAWK

Twenty-first century accommodations in Kitty Hawk are more abundant and more elaborate than what Wilbur and Orville Wright found when they traveled to the Outer Banks in the early 1900s to test their flying machine. Although several chain hotels have popped up in recent years, mom-and-pop motels located steps from the ocean remain a Kitty Hawk staple. Despite taking a battering from a plethora of storms over the years, these lodges continue to provide an old-school Outer Banks vacation experience to their guests.

JOURNEY'S END. This was the first motel travelers arriving from the north came to after exiting the Wright Memorial Bridge. Opened in 1952 by Basil M. Wells of Baltimore, Maryland, each of the motel's eight units had a living room, kitchenette, two bedrooms, and a bathroom. Journey's End expanded in 1955 to include a restaurant with seating for 200 guests. It was torn down in the late 1980s.

KAY-GENE COTTAGES. Gene and Kay Harrington owned the pink cottages at Milepost 3 in the 1960s and 1970s.

BUCCANEER. This 19-unit motel, located between Mileposts 5 and 6, opened in 1958. After owning the motel for two decades, David and Sandra Briggman transformed it into a drug and alcohol rehabilitation facility called Changing Tides Treatment Center in 2016.

SALT-AIRE COURT (SALTAIRE COTTAGES). Joseph and Lucille Stokes opened this cottage court at Milepost 2.5 in the 1950s. The establishment is still in operation today, offering guests two, three, and four-bedroom cottages as well as a swimming pool.

SEA KOVE. Lionel and Melba Beacham Shannon opened this motel at Milepost 3 in 1952, adding to it in 1953 and 1954. An Esther Williams–style pool, one of only two on the Outer Banks with a ledge for swimmers to walk on in the deep end, was installed in 1955. The motel lost two oceanfront cottages during the 1962 Ash Wednesday Storm and two more in 1972. The Shannons sold the motel to William Foreman in 1976. Foreman and his wife, Cari, added a row of apartments to the motel in 1977 and built a cabana, which was destroyed during Hurricane Isabel in 2003. The Sea Kove continues to welcome many guests who annually visit at the same time, including a 103-year-old Pennsylvania woman who in 2019 extended her record of staying at the motel each year since its opening. (Both, courtesy of William and Cari Foreman.)

SEA KOVE BONFIRE. For years, the highlight of many guests' week at the Sea Kove was the Friday night bonfire on the beach. The festivities kicked off with Sea Kove owner William Foreman picking up children staying at the motel in the back of his truck and driving them across the street to the beach to roast marshmallows over a blazing fire. (Both, courtesy of William and Cari Foreman.)

SOUTHERN SHORES MOTOR LODGE. After the 1962 Ash Wednesday Storm devastated the original Sea Ranch, a group of businessmen, including author David Stick, purchased the property and refurbished the northern annex of the motel as the Southern Shores Motor Lodge. Oil tycoon and Elizabeth City native Walter R. Davis and his Kitty Hawk Land Company purchased the property in the mid-1970s. The lodge later closed and was burned by local volunteer firefighters in a practice fire in 1985. Today, a Hilton Garden Inn sits on the site.

Five

ROANOKE ISLAND

Although the beaches with their cool Atlantic breezes have always been the Outer Banks' major attraction, more than a few visitors prefer to spend their nights away from the sound of ocean waves breaking on shore, opting instead to stay on Roanoke Island.

Today, guests seeking accommodations on Roanoke Island can choose from an array of bed-and-breakfasts as well as a few long-standing motels. In some ways, the accommodations reflect what visitors found a century ago—comfortable rooms, hearty meals, and gracious Southern hospitality—mixed with 21st-century amenities like flat-screen televisions, Wi-Fi, and DVD players.

Early Roanoke Island lodging establishments included the Roanoke Hotel, which Nathaniel Gould opened on Main and Water Streets in Manteo, in June 1899. Inventor Reginald Fessenden and his party stayed at the hotel in 1902 while conducting experiments that led to the transmission of wireless telephone messages across the water. The building that housed the hotel was destroyed in a February 1952 fire.

Gould also purchased the Tranquil House, adjacent to the Roanoke Hotel. Built in 1885, the inn advertised rooms for 25¢ per night and meals for 50¢ during the 1920s. It has been reimagined for modern travelers in the form of the Tranquil House Inn, designed in the style of 19th-century Outer Banks inns.

THE TRANQUIL HOUSE. Operated as a hotel and rooming house for nearly 70 years, the Tranquil House was established by W.D. Chadwick, one of Dare County's founders. It was later acquired by Asa V. Evans, who sold it to Nathaniel E. Gould in the 1920s. After Gould's death, his widow and four daughters, including Phoebe Gould Hayman, owner of the Arlington Hotel, sold the downtown property in 1950 to brothers M. Keith and W.B. Fearing, who owned the nearby Hotel Fort Raleigh. The Tranquil House was torn down in 1961. In 1964, a new Manteo Post Office was built on the inn's former site in downtown Manteo. (Courtesy of the Tranquil House Inn.)

THE TRANQUIL HOUSE INN. In 1988, the modern incarnation of the Tranquil House opened on the Manteo waterfront across the street from the site of the original inn. The inn's architecture combines elements of both the original inn and the Roanoke Hotel, a downtown lodge later converted to office space and destroyed by a fire in 1952. Along with a continental breakfast and wine reception, the Tranquil House offers the acclaimed 1587 Restaurant.

WHITE DOE INN. Listed in the National Register of Historic Places, the three-story White Doe Inn features nine guest rooms. Innkeepers Bob and Bebe Woody purchased the house from Goldie Meekins, the daughter-in-law of original owners Theodore and Rosa Meekins, in 1993 and opened it as a bed-and-breakfast. The Meekins family had moved to Manteo from Rodanthe in 1898 and completed construction on their house in 1910. The Queen Anne–style facade was inspired by a photograph in a Sears & Roebuck catalog. At the time, it was the largest house in Manteo.

FORT RALEIGH MOTOR COURT. Originally located opposite the entrance to Fort Raleigh, the Fort Raleigh Motor Court was initially a dance hall known as the Colonist Inn owned by Earl and Nora Mann. Manteo physician Dr. Wallace Harvey bought the units in the early 1960s and moved them down the road to the foot of the William B. Umstead Bridge. The motor court included two efficiencies rented by the month and nine single rooms rented by the day or week. The National Park Service purchased the property in 1990 and had area volunteer fire departments burn the remaining buildings in a controlled burn in 1994. (Courtesy of Elizabeth Granitzki.)

HOTEL FORT RALEIGH. Claude C. Duvall and C.D. Creef built the Hotel Fort Raleigh in downtown Manteo in 1931. Duvall later bought Creef out, and his wife, Mattie, ran the hotel. G.T. "Ras" Westcott Jr. leased the hotel from Duvall in 1940, and in 1942, brothers M. Keith and W.B. Fearing purchased it from Duvall. The Fort Raleigh Hotel closed in 1968 after 37 years in operation. It reopened as an apartment building in 1970 and later became the Dare County Administration Center. The building was torn down in 2019.

CANNADY'S GUESTHOUSE. Bernice Cannady was working at Manteo Furniture in 1941 when she heard that her dream house was for sale. She and her husband, Dan, purchased the downtown Manteo property and turned it into a guesthouse called Rest-Over Tourist Home. Boarders included traveling salesmen, fishermen, Civilian Conservation Corps workers, and tourists attending *The Lost Colony*. Cannady prepared breakfast and dinner for her guests. In the evenings, guests sat on the porch and listened to Cannady share information about the area. The home was one of two in Manteo with a four-gabled A-shaped roof. Bernice Cannady's granddaughter Melodye purchased the property after her grandmother died and continues to run it as a guesthouse. In this photograph, taken during the 1940s, Bernice and Dan Cannady's sons Dan Jr. (left) and Buddy (right) are sitting on the steps of the guesthouse with friend Alvah Ward in the middle. (Courtesy of Melodye Cannady.)

DARE HAVEN MOTEL. James M. Williams Sr. opened the Dare Haven Motel in the 1950s. Since then, every generation of the Williams family has served in the US military. The motel offers a discount to members of the military and first responders. (Author's collection.)

DUKE OF DARE MOTOR LODGE. The Duke of Dare Motor Lodge opened in the spring of 1964 on Highway 64 in Manteo. Owners of the 21-unit motel included George H. Creef, a partner in the Pioneer Theater, and Herbert A. Creef Jr., owner-operator of the Pioneer. The Duke of Dare has been closed since the early 2000s.

MANTEO MOTEL. Opened in 1954, this motel was owned by the Reverend Earl Meekins and family and run by Meekins's daughter and son-in-law, Ina and Burwell Evans. A restaurant was added in 1961. (Author's collection.)

ELIZABETHAN INN. An Elizabethan-styled addition to the Manteo Motel was built in 1966, the first of that design on Roanoke Island. Three years later, the restaurant was also remodeled in an Elizabethan design. Today, the 78-room motel is known as the Elizabethan Inn.

BIDE-A-WEE. Desmond and Doris Rogers began renting two rooms and a cabin in the backyard of their Manteo home to tourists in 1955. Guests from Scotland staying with the couple asked that the tourist home be named Bide-a-Wee, a Scottish saying meaning "stay a while." Andy Griffith, his wife, Barbara Edwards Griffith, and members of her family were among the first guests of the Bide-a-Wee Tourist Home and Cabins. A 10-room motel was added to the property in the early 1960s. Doris Rogers sold the motel in 1997. It is now known as the Island Guesthouse and Cottages. (Both, courtesy of Annette Rogers Jackson.)

BIDE-A-WEE TOURIST HOME AND CABINS

MRS. DORIS ROGERS

—— On Highway Above High School ——

Cool, Comfortable Rooms With Bath

HOT AND COLD WATER

Manteo, N. C. ———————— Tel. 111-W

```
CAMP CONTENTMENT, CROATAN SOUND, ROANOKE ISLAND
         Post Office Address, Box 55, Manteo, N. C.

This cottage is delightfully situated four miles from Manteo; modern roads. Telephone
at hand. Faces water and prevailing breezes. It has electric lights, water, complete
equipment, except linens and covers. Two double beds; two single beds. Pines. Sandy
beach for children. Excellent bathing at the door. Room for servant.
Available ..................................194....... to ....................................194............
Full week $........................................ no rates for shorter period.
            Address: VICTOR MEEKINS, P. O. Box 55, MANTEO, N. C.
```

CAMP CONTENTMENT. Located four miles from Manteo, this 1940s Roanoke Island waterfront establishment advertised electric lights and a sandy beach for children.

ROANOKE ISLAND MOTEL. The Roanoke Island Motel was located midway between Manteo and Fort Raleigh on a site where the Island Farm now stands. Roxie Etheridge Atkinson was the owner-operator.

CAMERON HOUSE INN. This 1919 Arts and Crafts bungalow has been restored as a bed and breakfast in downtown Manteo. The six guest rooms are decorated to evoke island living of yesteryear. (Author's collection.)

Six
HATTERAS ISLAND

While grand hotels emerged alongside motels and cottage courts on the northern Outer Banks during the mid-20th century, Hatteras Island's early accommodations were mainly hunting and fishing lodges. Soon, however, locals discovered tourism's profitability, and mom-and-pop motels began appearing along the narrow strand from Rodanthe to Hatteras. Many of them have closed in recent years, victims of hurricanes and other storms that have relentlessly battered the island. Others have survived nature's wrath, with their owners rebuilding units washed away by an angry sea to continue to offer simple yet comfortable accommodations.

TOWER CIRCLE MOTEL. Jack and Mary Gray and their daughter Jackie opened the 22-unit motel in 1958 near the Cape Hatteras Lighthouse. It originally included another building that was later demolished and eight apartments that became long-term rental units. Longtime Outer Banks visitors Earl and Gayle Johnson purchased the motel from the Gray family in 2012. Today, there are 11 units in the one-story, L-shaped brick building, which remains in operation despite repeated buffeting from storms.

THE SEA GULL MOTEL. Carlos and Josephine Oden opened the seven-room Sea Gull Motel in Hatteras Village in 1955. The motel grew to include 45 rooms, but most were washed away during Hurricane Isabel in 2003. Jeff Oden, the son of the original owners, and his wife, Katie, rebuilt the Sea Gull with 15 rooms. The family sold the property to SAGA Construction in 2016. (Author's collection.)

ODEN'S HARBOR MOTEL. The Oden family built this motel and Oden's Dock in Hatteras Village in the early 1950s. Harold Midgett later purchased the motel, and it was known as the Hatteras Harbor Motel until 2005. The Oden family, including the fifth generation, again owns the property, now called the Breakwater Inn, which was renovated in 2016. The inn's Fisherman's Quarters was part of the original motel.

ATLANTIC VIEW HOTEL. Hatteras Island's oldest hotel, the Atlantic View, opened in 1928 and operated until 2003, when it was closed after being heavily damaged during Hurricane Isabel. The hotel was refurbished and reopened with 10 guest rooms in 2006 as the Seaside Inn.

THE FALCON MOTEL. Ike Jennette owned and operated this 1960s-era Buxton motel. Longtime Hatteras Island vacationers Robert and Laura Handlow recently purchased and are renovating the property, which they have renamed the Swell Motel. (Author's collection.)

CAPE SANDBOX MOTEL. This Buxton motel was located a quarter-mile north of the Cape Hatteras Lighthouse.

LIGHTHOUSE VIEW COURT. John and Annie Hooper and their son Edgar opened the Lighthouse View Court in 1952 with three efficiencies. By the mid-1960s, the Buxton motel had expanded to 30 units. Its name was changed to Lighthouse View Motel in 1972. Edgar Hooper's son John took over the motel in 1976. Damaged during Hurricane Emily in 1993, the motel was restored, and today the property is known as Lighthouse View Oceanfront Lodging.

ORANGE BLOSSOM INN. Opened in the early 1950s, this Buxton motel took its name from orange trees that grew on the property. It advertised one- and two-bedroom apartments as well as a front-porch swing. After owner Walter Barnett died in 1974, his family sold the business, and the new owners converted it into a bakery. It is now known as the Orange Blossom Bakery & Café.

HATTERAS ISLAND MOTEL. Opened in 1964 in Rodanthe, the Hatteras Island Motel included a 1,000-foot fishing pier and a drive-in restaurant. It was torn down in the early 2000s.

Cape Hatteras Motel. A Buxton fixture since the late 1940s, the Cape Hatteras Motel was originally known as Cape Hatteras Court. The property was the first motel on Hatteras Island to feature a swimming pool. After purchasing the motel in 1971, the Dawson family renovated it and changed its name to Cape Hatteras Motel in 1975. Today, 37 units make up the Cape Hatteras Motel. (Both, courtesy of David Dawson.)

CAPE PINES MOTEL. Opened in 1953 and named for the canopy of pine trees marking the Buxton landscape, Cape Pines Motel was one of Hatteras Island's first motels. Original owner Leona Jennette managed the motel until selling it in the early 1980s. Current owners William and Angie Rapant purchased it in 2006. (Both, courtesy of William Rapant.)

BUXTON LANDMARK. The Cape Pines Motel has been expanded over the years to include a main two-story building with 15 rooms, the registration lobby, and a common area. In recent years, the courtyard rooms have been restored to their original state with hardwood floors and knotty-pine ceilings. The motel's pool was also recently renovated. (Courtesy of William Rapant.)

OUTER BANKS MOTEL. This motel had three units when William and Carol White Dillon opened it in 1955. Eleven more units were added to the Buxton establishment by the end of the decade. Carol Dillon's family has lived on Hatteras Island for generations, and her pre-adolescent life was the basis for Nell Wise Wechter's book *Taffy of Torpedo Junction*. An Outer Banks native, Wechter had been Dillon's seventh-grade teacher and had lived with her family while teaching school on the island.

DURANT MOTOR COURT. Andrew Shanklin "Shank" and Ruby Austin opened the 30-room Durant Motor Court in the early 1950s. The property was destroyed during Hurricane Isabel in 2003.

GENERAL BILLY MITCHELL MOTEL. Andrew Shanklin "Shank" and Ruby Austin also owned this motel, named for Brig. Gen. William "Billy" Mitchell, who devised an experiment off Cape Hatteras in 1923 to determine if high-level bombs could sink battleships. After being ravaged by Hurricane Isabel in 2003, the motel was closed and razed. The site where it sat is now part of the Hatteras Island Ocean Center.

HATTERAS MARLIN MOTEL. Built in 1964, the motel included 39 rooms, four efficiencies, and three suites. Flooded during Hurricane Matthew in 2016, it was subsequently closed and razed.

OCEAN AIRE MOTEL. Located on the Pamlico Sound in Rodanthe, this motel opened in the 1970s, but after taking a battering from storms, it closed in the 2000s.

BURRUS MOTOR COURT. Situated directly across from Hatteras Harbor, this motel opened in the early 1950s and began falling into disrepair after being hammered by Hurricane Isabel in 2003. Following the death of owner David Burrus in late 2018, the property now sits abandoned.

FULLER'S MOTEL. Local business and civic leader George Fuller owned this Buxton motel and cottage court in the 1950s and 1960s. It later became a bed-and-breakfast.

Seven

OCRACOKE

Settled in the 1700s, Ocracoke Island began attracting mainland visitors by the end of the century. During the late 1800s, wealthy mainland North Carolina residents, especially hunters and fishermen, boarded steamships to travel to Ocracoke, where they stayed at the village's large Victorian hotel, known as the Ponder, or Ponzer.

Increasing numbers of vacationers discovered the island during the 20th century thanks to the introduction of electricity in 1938, the paving of the first roads in 1942, and the establishment of a ferry service in 1950. Telephone service, a municipal water system, and internet access also came to the island. Despite these advances, visitors still find a quaint, relaxed atmosphere on Ocracoke. It is only accessible by ferry, private boat, or plane, and bicycles and golf carts are the preferred modes of transportation around the island.

Tourism is the island's main economic driver, but the industry suffered significant losses after Hurricane Dorian churned up the Pamlico Sound in September 2019. The small island was inundated with record flooding. At least 80 percent of the homes of Ocracoke's 950 fulltime residents suffered significant damage. As residents and property owners clean up and rebuild, they are determined to restore the island and its vital tourism industry.

HOTEL PONDER,
OCRACOKE, N. CAR.

This is an all-the-year-round resort, and the coming season promises to be the best for many. The table will be supplied with the best the market affords. Fish, clams, oysters and crabs are abundant. The rooms are cleanly, and there is always a salt breeze from some point. The island is between the Atlantic Ocean and Pamlico Sound, and the nearest point to the main land is twenty miles; hence there is no land breeze, and the atmosphere is free from malaria.

There will be a good band of music constantly on hand, and the pleasure and comfort of the guests will be carefully looked after. Serf-bathing, sailing, fishing and dancing will be the chief amusements. This is one of the best points on the Atlantic coast for the sporting angleman.

The steamer Virginia Dare, of the Old Dominion Line, will make two trips a week from Washington, leaving Saturday nights and returning Sunday nights, and leaving Wednesday mornings and returning Thursday nights, touching at all points touched on her regular trips. The E. C. D. Line steamer between Newbern and Elizabeth City will touch at that point both ways. The mid-week trip of the Virginia Dare will be a day trip, and a most pleasant one on the seaworthy and handsomely furnished steamer. The officers are polite and courteous.

RATES AT HOTEL PONDER:—From $7 to $10 per week; children and nurses half price. For rates by the month or for large parties, address GEORGE CREDLE, Prop'r, OCRACOKE, N. C.

HOTEL PONDER. Seeking a reasonably priced summer vacation place for their families, a group of businessmen opened a large Victorian establishment called the Ocracoke Hotel in 1885. Built in the shape of a Roman cross, the lodge was later renamed the Ponder Hotel and became the center of summer entertainment on the island. The hotel survived a powerful August 1899 storm only to be destroyed by a fire in the spring of 1900. The blaze began when hotel owner George Credle and a boat captain left a goose cooking atop an unattended Wilson heater. The pot boiled over, and the resulting flames quickly engulfed the hotel. The location where the hotel stood is now underwater between the former Coast Guard station and the mouth of Silver Lake. This ad for the hotel appeared in the June 23, 1897, issue of the *Washington (North Carolina) Progress*.

THE ANCHORAGE INN AND MARINA. Overlooking Silver Lake Harbor, this four-story, 35-room motel is the island's tallest building (not including the lighthouse). In addition, there are two fifth-floor suites. The motel stands on the former site of a house owned by David Williams, the first chief of the US Coast Guard station on Ocracoke Island. The Williams house was moved down the street and is now the home of the Ocracoke Preservation Society. (Courtesy of the Ocracoke Preservation Society.)

ISLAND INN. Built in 1901, the Island Inn was originally the site of the Ocracoke Odd Fellows Lodge on its upper floor and the Ocracoke School on the first floor. As an inn, it was initially called the Hotel Silver Lake. After falling into disrepair in recent years, much of the hotel and restaurant was demolished in 2019. The Ocracoke Preservation Society, which owns the property, plans to restore the building's center section for use as a visitors' center. (Courtesy of the Ocracoke Preservation Society.)

WAHAB VILLAGE HOTEL. Ocracoke native Robert Stanley Wahab opened the island's first modern hotel in 1936. Ocracoke's first facility with electricity, the hotel boasted a movie theater, skating rink, and kitchen that served family-style meals. One of the first to envision Ocracoke as a tourist spot, Wahab was responsible for bringing the first telephone switchboard, first ice plant, and first commuter airplane service to Ocracoke. He also pushed for ferry service to Ocracoke from Hatteras and Cedar Island and ensured that the island had telephone and mail service and paved roads. Wahab's great-grand-nephew Stanley "Chip" Stevens and his wife, Helena, purchased the hotel in 2007 and operate it as Blackbeard's Lodge. (Courtesy of the Ocracoke Preservation Society.)

WAHAB EXPANSION. Over the years, Robert Stanley Wahab expanded his Wahab Village Hotel to include a campground, a hunting and fishing club, cottages, and a dinner and dancing club known as the Spanish Casino. (Courtesy of the Ocracoke Preservation Society.)

PONY ISLAND MOTEL. Opened in 1958, the Pony Island Motel has been owned and operated by the Esham family since 1973. Island natives David Scott and Melinda Esham became the owners in 2004. The 50-unit motel includes 5 suites, 4 efficiencies, and 41 rooms. (Above, courtesy of Pony Island Motel; below, courtesy of the Ocracoke Preservation Society.)

EDWARDS OF OCRACOKE. Wayne and Trudy Clark have owned Edwards of Ocracoke since 1996. Originally part of the Wahab Village Inn, the establishment includes 11 rooms and efficiencies, six cottage apartments, and two private cottages. During World War II, what were known as the lodge's green apartments housed military members watching for German submarines. (Both, courtesy of Trudy Clark.)

BERKELEY MANOR. Hyde County native Sam Jones moved to Norfolk, Virginia, where he obtained a job at Berkeley Machine Works and Foundry Company. Six years later, Jones purchased the company. He came to Ocracoke in 1939 with his first wife, a native of the island, and built Berkeley Manor as a place for visiting friends and business associates to stay. Since 2012, the estate has been used as an events venue and lodging establishment. (Courtesy of the Ocracoke Preservation Society.)

THE CASTLE. When Berkeley Manor was unable to accommodate all of his guests, Sam Jones built Berkeley Castle. In 1997, David Escham and Steve Wright opened the Castle as a bed-and-breakfast. The property includes 12 guest rooms in the main house and nine villas. (Courtesy of the Ocracoke Preservation Society.)

SILVER LAKE MOTEL & INN. Edward and Jean Wrobleski and their six children visited Ocracoke Island in the late 1970s and purchased property on Silver Lake where they built the Silver Lake Motel & Inn. It is the second-tallest building on Ocracoke Island (not including the lighthouse). (Author's collection.)

BLUFF SHOAL MOTEL. Van Henry and Bertha O'Neal opened the Bluff Shoal Motel overlooking Silver Lake in 1966. The motel takes its name from a shoal in Pamlico Sound located halfway between Ocracoke and Cedar Island. Wayne and Jennifer Garrish, the motel's fourth owners, purchased the property in 1994. (Courtesy of Wayne Garrish.)

PAMLICO INN. Built on the Pamlico Sound in the late 1800s, the Pamlico Inn became a popular spot for hunters and fishermen. The inn was destroyed during a hurricane in 1944. (Courtesy of the Ocracoke Preservation Society.)

SOUND FRONT INN. Elisha Chase built the original portion of the inn on Lighthouse Road overlooking the Pamlico Sound in the late 1820s. It was known as the Cedar Grove Inn during the 1930s and as Sound Front Inn after Warwick T. and Margaret Boos purchased it in 1951. In recent years, it has been used as a rental cottage. (Courtesy of the Ocracoke Preservation Society.)

OCRACOKE HARBOR INN. The Miller family has owned and operated the inn overlooking Silver Lake since 1998. Ocracoke Harbor Inn includes 16 rooms and eight suites, and five cottages are located throughout the island. Its office on Silver Lake was refurbished after being damaged during flooding from Hurricane Dorian. (Author's collection.)

THURSTON HOUSE INN. Built in the early 1920s, the Thurston House was the home of Capt. Tony Thurston Gaskill. His daughter and son-in-law, Marlene and Randal Mathews, opened the house as a bed-and-breakfast in 1996 and built a guesthouse next door in 1999. Marlene Mathews's sister, Donna Boor, purchased the inn in 2005. Boor and her mother, Annie Louise Gaskill Gaskins, run the Thurston House Inn, which is listed in the National Register of Historic Places. (Author's collection.)

SAND DOLLAR MOTEL. Grady and Mamie Bridgers of Landis, North Carolina, opened the establishment in 1959, naming it the Ocracoke Motel. In addition to undergoing a name change over the years, the motel has changed hands several times and has been expanded to include 11 rooms, an efficiency, and a cottage. Rick and Jill Gunter purchased the property in 2015. Although the cottage and the motel's first-floor rooms were damaged during flooding from Hurricane Dorian, the Gunters plan to reopen for the summer of 2020. (Courtesy of Jill Gunter.)

WAGON WHEELS COTTAGES. Daisy Styron Gaskill opened this cottage court in 1957. Operated by the Gaskill family for more than 40 years, the cottages suffered extensive damage during Hurricane Dorian. (Author's collection.)

Visit us at
arcadiapublishing.com

www.ingramcontent.com/pod-product-compliance
Lightning Source LLC
Chambersburg PA
CBHW060937170426
43194CB00027B/2982